THE GIVING LIFE

WHY IT IS MORE BLESSED
TO GIVE THAN TO RECEIVE

THE
GIVING
LIFE

WHY IT IS MORE BLESSED
TO GIVE THAN TO RECEIVE

DAVID H. ROSEBERRY

RML BOOKS
PLANO, TEXAS

ISBN Paperback 978-1-7358461-3-2
ISBN eBook 978-1-7358461-4-9

Book cover design by David Roseberry and BluDesign, Nashville, TN

Photo by Claudio Schwarz on Unsplash

Interior design by YouPublish (youpublish.com)

Published by RML Books, 4545 Charlemagne Drive, Plano, Texas 75093
www.RMLBooks.com

Printed in the United States of America

For those generous believers who gave willingly to the ministry God called us to do. I know you have discovered that it is more blessed to give than receive.

TABLE OF CONTENTS

PREFACE

A few years ago, as a spiritual discipline, I decided I would stand at my desk and read aloud all of Paul's letters in the New Testament. I had studied the Apostle's letters before, of course. Over a span of three decades, as the Senior Pastor of my church, I had taught and preached through most of the letters of Paul and the history of his mission and ministry from the Acts of the Apostles. During my ministry, I became well-acquainted with the biblical theology of the great Apostle.

However, I had not read the letters *as letters;* as personal, pastoral heart-felt correspondence from a leader of the church to a new congregation of people he loved and cared about. I knew that his letters were read aloud to the churches to which they are addressed, but I had never read them that way. I had not read them aloud in their entirety. In other words, I had read them, but I hadn't *heard* them.

This point should not be lost on us. When the church in Corinth, Greece received a letter from Paul, they would not have passed out individual copies of it for all to read at home in their living room the way we do now. Instead, the letter would have been read to them. The church would have gathered, and an elder or leader would have unrolled the heavy parchment on which the letter was written, cleared his throat, and opened his mouth to speak. The people would have listened to a public reading from a letter from Paul.

I had never heard an entire letter read aloud—and I had never read one aloud either. I felt that I was missing some authenticity.

So, one afternoon, when I was by myself at home, I opened the Bible on the desk in my study and I turned to the two letters of Paul to the Corinthians. I imagined myself standing before a small group of church members. Did they meet in a room? In a home? Did they gather under a tree? It didn't matter; they were all there as I imagined. I cleared my throat and began. I read aloud both letters of Paul to the Corinthian church as if to an assembled group gathered to hear the latest admonishment from Paul.

I understood them in an entirely new way.

Paul gets a bad reputation for being too, well, Paul-like. He is unquestionably forceful. He lays it down on the line for the members of the early church. He doesn't pull his punches. He has strong opinions. There are significant problems in this young church, and Paul does not mince his words in correcting them.

But behind the sometimes-fiery rhetoric and rebuke, Paul shows something else. Paul loved the members of the church. He had been in Corinth for eighteen months to start the congregation. He had worked among the people supporting himself as a tent maker. He understood the culture of the local community. The locals gave Paul ample reason to rebuke them; they were steeped in sin, and much of their behavior was incompatible with the Christian faith that Paul proclaimed. But behind the words and warnings was a heart of love for the people.

I was particularly surprised by how frank Paul was in teaching these early Christians about giving—about stewardship and generosity. That is where this book came from. It is my pastoral commentary on the wisdom and words of the Apostle Paul about the Giving Life.

I hope it will be helpful to you as a church member, or a church leader, or a pastor.

I have written several other books using the same style of text, reflection, and application. I invite you to read *When the Lord Is My Shepherd, The Psalm on the Cross, The Ordinary Ways of God,* and others of my books that can be purchased through Amazon.

David H. Roseberry

life of faith? Most of the instructions and teaching that Paul gives in his letters is doctrinal and theological. He shows us how to live a right and moral life. But he is also clear about how we should think about our money. In chapters 8 and 9, he addresses the topics of money, giving, generosity, how we should give—and even how much we should give! More to the point, Paul shows us what giving looks like when we are faithful citizens of the Kingdom of God.

The Giving Life addresses the critical need that believers have to get their thinking, theology, and practices about money and possessions in line with Biblical teaching. We all live in a 'me-oriented' culture. Our temptation to focus on things, goods, resources, income, funds, assets, property, possessions, and personal wealth comes to us very naturally. This is not the way of the Lord Jesus, as we know. And the early Christians knew this as well. Indeed, the first Christians knew the Lord's teaching on giving and generosity. They knew it well. Paul's statement at the end of his speech to the elders in Miletus was a simple reminder of this: "Remember the words of the Lord Jesus how He said: *'It is more blessed to give than to receive!'*"[1]

THE GIVING LIFE AND YOU

Two thousand years ago, the Holy Spirit empowered Paul's words, and the Holy Spirit empowered those words again

---

1. This remarkable verse from Acts 20:35 is not written in the Gospel accounts. However, it was a well-known statement understood to be the clear and comprehensive teaching of the Lord Jesus. Every Christian appears to have known the phrase by heart—which we do today as well. And like today, the early Christians needed some help to remember it.

in my life. I hope that you will find, as you study and "go deep" with the Apostle, that the Holy Spirit empowers these words for you as well.

You will love what you hear from the Apostle Paul. His teaching is chock-full of simple, applicable truths that can make a huge material difference in your life. But we must first understand his audience—the people among whom he lived, worked, ministered, and preached. Who were the people in Corinth whom he loved?

WHO WERE THE CORINTHIANS?

The early members of the Corinthian Church were a mixed group of people. They came from all kinds of backgrounds. There were Greeks, Romans, and Jews who were the first members of the church. There were sailors, fishermen, weavers, builders, slaves, freedmen, city officials, and ladies of the evening who regularly attended their public worship services. Some were wealthy members—rich enough to own businesses, travel for sales, or have streets in the city of Corinth named after them. Many were working-class who, like Paul, labored with their hands or their backs. Some were quite poor. Among the members of the church were people who had been wounded sexually, relationally, and emotionally. There were a few named souls who seemed to have their lives together. Many were simply hanging on.

But they were all members of the same church and, for better or for worse, they were trying to follow Jesus as their Lord the very best they could. This mixed bag of a congregation makes it more surprising that Paul has something to say to all of them—as one body of Christ. He does not single out the rich. He does not segment the middle-income earners. He does not exclude the poor. For everyone at Corinth, the promise is made—giving will bring joy, it will increase faith, it will challenge others, it will do good, it will stretch our faith, and it will make us confident of the goodness and provision of God.

WHAT'S IN THIS BOOK?

We will begin the book with an excerpt from the Second Letter of Paul to the Corinthians, chapters 8 and 9. It will be formatted as it if were a memo to the church.

Then each of the following short chapters begins with a snippet or verse from the Second Letter of Paul to the Corinthians, or perhaps from the Book of the Acts of the Apostles. The following commentary is designed for your reflection and further thought in the context of your personal prayer, small group meeting, family discussion over dinner, or any other venue you can imagine.

The biblical text cited before each chapter is taken from the English Standard Version of the New Testament. Some passages, where noted, some from the New International Version of the Bible.

The words that follow are my own thoughts and commentary on Paul's letter to the Corinthians.

Additionally, when I had completed this book, I read through it one more time as if I were attending a small group study with this book as its curriculum. I imagined what kind of questions I would either want to ask of others, answer myself, or open for discussion. The questions that end each chapter came relatively easily to me—as your own comments and questions would come easily to you. Feel free to use the printed questions or write your own. The Giving Life and the subject of giving, stewardship, generosity, and money is endlessly fascinating and applicable. Have at it!

Over many years, I have learned volumes from so many friends and colleagues about the subject of generosity and giving, but I must call out one of my friends and colleagues, Kolby Kerr. Several years ago, he helped me pull these thoughts together in many ways. He has an eye for editing, writing, and organization. I give him full honors for the substantial work he did a few years ago in preparing a much shorter version of the same subject. And, as I reviewed, reworked, and rewrote this edition, I realized I had forgotten which thoughts were original to me or to him.

Generosity, as you will see in the pages ahead, is very personal. Whatever we give away says a great deal about us, our possessions, our age in life and our stage in life, how we were raised, and what we ultimately put our faith and trust in. I hope this commentary can provide guidance and insight as you consider your generosity in light of the Scripture and the heart of the Apostle Paul.

May the Grace of God be with you as you read this book.

David H. Roseberry
Summer 2022

A MEMORANDUM TO THE CHURCH IN CORINTH

From: The Apostle Paul
To: The Christian Church in Corinth

We want you to know, brothers, about the grace of God that has been given among the churches of Macedonia, for in a severe test of affliction, their abundance of joy and their extreme poverty have overflowed in a wealth of generosity on their part. For they gave according to their means, as I can testify, and beyond their means, of their own accord, begging us earnestly for the favor of taking part in the relief of the saints—and this, not as we expected, but they gave themselves first to the Lord and then by the will of God to us. Accordingly, we urged Titus that as he had started, so he should complete among you this act of grace. But as you excel in everything—in faith, in speech, in knowledge, in all earnestness, and in our love for you—see that you excel in this act of grace also.

I say this not as a command, but to prove by the earnestness of others that your love also is genuine. For you know the grace of our Lord Jesus Christ, that though he was rich, yet for your sake he became poor, so that you by his poverty might become rich. And in this matter, I give my judgment: this benefits you, who a year ago started not only to do this work but also to desire to do it. So now finish doing it as well, so that your readiness in desiring it may be matched by your completing it out of what you have. For if the readiness is there, it is acceptable according to what a person has, not according to what he does not have. For I do not mean that others should be eased, and you burdened, but that as a matter of fairness your abundance at the present time should supply their need, so that their abundance may supply your need, that there may be fairness. (Based on 2 Corinthians 8:1–14)

The point is this: whoever sows sparingly will also reap sparingly, and whoever sows bountifully will also reap bountifully. Each one must give as he has decided in his heart, not reluctantly or under compulsion, for God loves a cheerful giver. And God is able to make all grace abound to you, so that having all sufficiency in all things at all times, you may abound in every good work.

He who supplies seed to the sower and bread for food will supply and multiply your seed for sowing and increase the harvest of your righteousness. You will be enriched in every way to be generous in every way, which through us will produce thanksgiving to God. For the ministry of this service is not only supplying the needs of the saints but is also overflowing in many thanksgivings to God. By their approval of this service, they will glorify God because of your submission that comes from your confession of the gospel of Christ, and the generosity of your contribution for them and for all others, while they long for you and pray for you, because of the surpassing grace of God upon you. Thanks be to God for his inexpressible gift! (Based on 2 Corinthians 9:6–15)

"We want you to know . . ."
2 Corinthians 8:1 (ESV)

. . . .

1. THE GIVING LIFE

"We want you to know . . ." 2 Corinthians 8:1

I n his second letter to the Corinthians, Paul delivers some of the most practical and powerful teaching on Christian generosity in the Bible. To those who had known him earlier in his life, this sentence would have been complete nonsense. Saul of Tarsus? Writing to Gentile Christians? About giving money? This must be a case of mistaken identity!

In a sense, that's exactly what it was. Paul had been given a new identity altogether. As a result of his dramatic Damascus Road conversion, the young Pharisee was so closely touched by Jesus that he would later say he had been "crucified with Christ." Paul, in his dramatic way of describing himself, no longer lived. Paul explained this in a letter to the Galatians. He said that Christ was now living in him instead of himself. His identity changed. His statement is powerful enough to quote here.

> *It is no longer I who live, but Christ who lives in me. And the life I now live in the*

> *flesh I live by faith in the Son of God, who
> loved me and gave himself for me.*
>
> *Galatians 2:20*

Jesus had given His life for Paul. And, in turn, Paul was giving Him his life in return. He became a giver.

As we read the verses from 2 Corinthians 8–9 together, we will see that, for Paul, it was the giving life of Jesus Christ that revealed the heart of God, transformed lives, and that testified to the whole world the power of the kingdom of God. The gospel he brought with him throughout the world wasn't mere words. It wasn't an intellectual game. There were real world ramifications for what Jesus had done on the cross. Paul saw himself as a chief spokesman, ambassador, emissary, and apologist for the Lord.

All this change was brought about by the self-giving life of Jesus who had spoken to Paul on that road. From that moment on, Paul gave his life to the Lord. He told the Philippians, "I press on to take hold of that for which Christ Jesus took hold of me" (Philippians 3:12, NIV).

Many of us have a story like this too, albeit maybe not as dramatic, or as passionate. But if you are reading this short book, you understand this. You have been touched by God. You have encountered Jesus Christ. You have been moved by the Holy Spirit. Or maybe you are just beginning a journey to discover if the Christian faith is true. I pray you will discover the truth soon enough.

But for now, we can think about Paul. He is the author of this love letter to the Christians in Corinth. He is the missionary who was so touched by the giving life of Jesus that he invited others into living out a Giving Life of their own.

Looking Back:

1. Think about Paul for a minute. He had a complete change of mind on the road to Damascus. Few of us have ever had such a conversion. Have you had a "change of mind" about Jesus?

2. Paul writes, "It is no longer I who live, but Christ who lives in me." Express this in your own words. What does it mean?

"Now as Saul went on his way, he approached Damascus, and suddenly a light from heaven shone around him." Acts 9:3

. . . .

2. THE UNLIKELIEST APOSTLE

"Now as Saul went on his way, he approached Damascus, and suddenly a light from heaven shone around him."
Acts 9:3

Before we take our deep dive into Paul's words to the Corinthians, we need to reacquaint ourselves with his story. We should begin by calling him Saul, the Pharisee of Tarsus. Here was a man of colossal intellect, with an unmatched zeal for his religion, who radically opposed this new fringe group of "Christians" who (in his mind) had defiled his faith.

Paul was whole-heartedly against Christianity. He was a religious fanatic who carried out acts of violence against those he viewed as infidels. In our modern vocabulary, we would have called Saul a terrorist. He presided over the death of Stephen and was "ravaging the church, and entering house after house, he dragged off men and women and committed them to prison" (Acts 8:3).

Then, on an assignment to arrest and harass Christians, while traveling on a road to Damascus, everything changed. He met the object of his scorn, Jesus, and was instantly reborn. Skeptics may doubt this miraculous encounter with the risen Jesus, but what is beyond any debate is what happened next. Saul was a changed man, and the course of history changed along with him.

This encounter with Jesus took Saul's world apart. Physically, he was left blind and unable to speak or eat for days. But imagine the much deeper losses he suffered in that moment: everything he'd ever believed in, taken pride in, or worked toward, went up in smoke. His substantial personal achievements were all worthless now. Worse than worthless—his greatest work (terrorizing followers of Christ) was now his greatest shame, a sign of his stupidity and sin!

Everything fell apart at Jesus' question: why are you persecuting Me? Jesus asks Saul where he's headed, what he's working for. And suddenly, in the stark light of Christ's glory, Saul had no idea.

Saul may have been the unlikeliest apostle, but it is very likely that all of us have experienced a moment like this. Some of us would say that when we first recognized who Jesus is and what He has done, we felt everything else fall away. We became aware of the futility of our own pursuits and the joy of finally finding our true purpose in God.

Let's thank the Lord for the work He did in the great Apostle Paul. He wants to do a similar work in all of us. What if He is already at work in us, whether we know it or not?

Looking Back:

1. Paul was instantly reborn on the road to Damascus. Do you relate to his sudden conversion, or has your faith come to you over time?
2. Do you believe that God is already at work in you? What are you learning? In what area of life are you growing as a follower of Christ?

"So the disciples determined, every one according to his ability, to send relief to the brothers living in Judea. And they did so, sending it to the elders by the hand of Barnabas and Saul." Acts 11:29–30

3. MISSION GENEROSITY

"So the disciples determined, every one according to his ability, to send relief to the brothers living in Judea. And they did so, sending it to the elders by the hand of Barnabas and Saul." Acts 11:29–30

Following a timeline in the early church, we are still years away from Paul's visit to the Corinthians, but we are piecing together the reason why he was in Corinth in the first place.

Picture Paul in Antioch (modern day Syria), putting his world back together in the light of his encounter with Jesus on the road to Damascus. He then hears the words of a prophet named Agabus, who prophesies a great famine that will come upon the churches across Judea. The disciples decided to organize a financial collection to help these Christians, and the first one to volunteer to lead the fund-raising program for the Christians in Judea was none other than the one who had tried to kill or imprison them!

When we read of Paul's missionary journeys in the book of Acts, we marvel at the preaching, the persecution, the miracles, the churches that sprang up and flourished because of his faithful work. But consider something even more amazing. Remember the mission of the mission: to find funds to help the Christians in Jerusalem. The heart of Paul's mission was generosity—the disciples sent him to collect an offering for the sake of the suffering churches in Jerusalem. And, despite the obstacles, Paul collected an enormous gift to sustain those in need.

We sometimes think of giving money as something that happens aside from the act of worship. Or perhaps we think of it as just a technical necessity; after all, we've got to keep the lights on and the water running. But that's not what we will see in Paul's missionary journey. He did not separate generosity from the message of the gospel, and neither should we. Good News and good giving are inextricably linked together. If giving isn't a central part of our Christian life, we are missing out on a big part and significant blessing of the Christian life. The Christian life is, by definition, a Giving Life.

Pastor and author John Tyson, in his book "A Creative Minority" has offered a wonderful summary statement about the generosity of the first Christians. He draws a sharp distinction between the Greco-Roman world of greed, lust, and power and the common Christian behaviors of generosity, compassion, and grace. This is his quote-worthy summary:

> *"The Early Church was strikingly different from the culture around it in this way—the pagan society was stingy with its money and promiscuous with its body. A pagan gave nobody their money and practically*

gave everybody their body. And the Christians came along and gave practically nobody their body and they gave practically everybody their money."

This statement is a perfect summary of the ethic of the Early Church. They were generous. They lived the Giving Life.

It begs the question about our own levels of generosity, doesn't it?

Looking Back:

1. Do you think that giving money for the work of the church is an act of worship? How might that be true?
2. Re-read the quote from John Tyson. What do you think of it?

"We want you to know,
brothers, about the
grace of God that has
been given among the
churches of Macedonia."
2 Corinthians 8:1

. . . .

4. DIRE STRAITS

"We want you to know, brothers, about the grace of God that has been given among the churches of Macedonia."
2 Corinthians 8:1

. . . .

As we take our deep dive into Paul's letter in chapters 8 and 9, we can see the heart and personality of the Apostle shine. He is going to have some fun at the expense of the Corinthians (literally!). He is going to tease them, push them a little bit, for their own good and the good of the cause. Follow the story.

Remember, Paul is taking up a collection for Christians in Jerusalem some 1500 miles away. In 2 Corinthians 8, we learn of the generosity of the Macedonian churches (these churches were located in Philippi, Berea, and Thessaloniki, all rival towns in the northern part of Greece). Paul highlighted the extraordinary giving of the northern Christians as a way of showing the relatively slow and stingy response of the Corinthians. We can think of Paul's statement to the Corinthians as a good-natured poke at their competitive spirit.

Do you remember the old pep rally chant meant to taunt an opposing team at a ballgame? "We've got spirit, yes, we do! We've got spirit, how 'bout you?" In essence, Paul says of these Macedonians, "They've got Spirit! Yes, they do!" and turns to the Corinthians and asks: "Okay, so how about you?"

But we shouldn't get the idea that these Macedonians were all that well off. They weren't sitting on heaps of cash from all their shrewd investments. There was something seriously bad going on in their community. Paul describes a "severe test of affliction," which could refer to a plague, famine, economic recession, or other disaster. Regardless, they were in trying circumstances and "extreme poverty." Sounds like the definition of hopelessness: grim circumstances and no resources to fall back on. It sounds like dire straits.

We don't know what had happened to these churches; we don't know what hardship afflicted them, but they were not living on Easy Street. Verse two is very revealing:

> *for in a severe test of affliction, their abundance*
> *of joy and their extreme poverty have overflowed*
> *in a wealth of generosity on their part.*

2 Corinthians 8:2

Their situation was severe. However, Paul doesn't paint a picture of hopelessness; instead, he says that it was in this precise moment that these churches showed "an abundance of joy" that "overflowed in a wealth of generosity."

From a worldly perspective, these phrases really shouldn't go anywhere near each other. Too often, we equate having an abundance of joy with having an abundance of stuff. Paul speaks, though, of a "wealth of generosity" that can flourish and overflow even during hardship and suffering.

I have called this church in Macedonia the "go-giver" church; as we will see, they were eager to be involved in the mission of God. They were generous. Later in the study, we will contrast this church with the church in Corinth who were the "go-getters" of the New Testament. They were eager to get more and more for themselves. This contrast is Paul's point!

And the contrast begs the question about our own Giving Life: in which church would we want to become members?

Looking Back:

1. What do you think about Paul comparing the giving of one church to the giving of another? Is this something that should be a regular practice?
2. What do you think are the attributes of a "Go-Giver" church vs. a "Go-Getter" church?

"We want you to know, brothers, about the grace of God that has been given among the churches of Macedonia."
2 Corinthians 8:1

. . . .

5. ENOUGH IS ENOUGH

"We want you to know, brothers, about the grace of God that has been given among the churches of Macedonia."
2 Corinthians 8:1

When Paul boasts of the generosity of the Macedonian churches, he isn't pretending that their ability to give generously originated with them. He says as much: *"We want you to know, brothers, about the grace of God that has been given among the churches of Macedonia."* These churches gave, not because they had discovered some secret formula or possessed some superpower, but because they had received generosity, they were now able to give.

It was the grace of God that moved them to give. They received grace and became gracious. This is the starting point for the Giving Life: we discover that the grace of God is real, and we *want* to become givers because of it.

We can think of these churches similarly to the people Jesus singles out in the Beatitudes in Matthew 5. Jesus runs through a list of the down and out—the poor, the meek, the persecuted—and pronounces them "blessed." In a sense, He calls them "lucky." To Jesus, the difficulty of their circumstances allowed them to be uniquely receptive to the generous work of God in their lives, which meant they received benefits that others walked right past. In this way, poverty isn't a barrier to generosity.

For many today, this would be a *non-sequitur*. It does not follow that someone who lives in poverty could be generous. In fact, there is something in us that pushes back on the idea of the poorest or hard-luck people giving from their stores. My mother used to say "Charity begins at home . . ." thinking she was quoting the Bible. But she wasn't. According to the Bible, the Giving Life is not about taking care of our needs first, and then giving out of what is left over. Instead, the Bible calls everyone, blessed or lucky or not, to be generous at home and with everyone else!

This is what is so remarkable about the Giving Life of the early Christians. When we remember that the Christians in Macedonia were giving for people in Judea some 1500 miles away—people whose names they did not know, people whose faces they would never see—when we remember this, we should be humbled by their generosity and their eagerness to give. Even if they did not have a perfect life with plenty of extras, they gave so that others might be cared for.

In other words, we shouldn't wait until we have enough to give enough. The Macedonians, who found joy in giving beyond themselves, should serve as an inspiration to us as well as a challenge. They've got Spirit. Yes, they do! How about you?

Is your life a ready receptacle for the generous grace of God? Because our ability to become generous people isn't measured by the size of our checking account. Our level of generosity will change the more we are changed by the grace of God.

Looking Back:

1. The grace of God motivated the Macedonians to give. What does that mean for us today?
2. Have you ever given money to help people that you will never see or meet? What is the motivation for this kind of giving?

"For they gave according to their means, as I can testify, and beyond their means . . ."
2 Corinthians 8:3

6. THEY WERE "GO-GIVERS"!

"For they gave according to their means, as I can testify, and beyond their means . . ." 2 Corinthians 8:3

But how on earth could such distressed people give anything, much less give enough to become the model of Christian generosity for all time? What does the Giving Life look like, in real terms?

The Macedonians were "go-givers"—for them, generosity wasn't a casual thing. Paul writes that they "gave according to their means." Those who could give a little, gave a little; those who could give more, gave more. They didn't just check for loose change when the plate was passed or give because they were guilted by some emotional appeal, and they didn't give whatever was left over once they'd paid the bills. These men and women made intentional decisions to give after prayerful consideration of what they had to offer.

We learn from Paul in his first letter to the Corinthians that there was a standard for the Christians. There was a template for every believing household to follow. It was called, "proportional giving." They gave according to their means. We will look at this later in the study, but we can mark it down as the standard practice for the New Testament believer. Giving was to be proportionate to their income.[2] It was built on a simple, powerful, but short, bumper-sticker-size idea: *Not equal gifts, but equal sacrifice.*

Jesus made it clear throughout his ministry that God cares about our hearts, and this is especially true when it comes to giving. There's no magic number that will earn you God's approval. God desires our prayerful obedience. He desires lives that are fully devoted to following him and that aren't holding anything back. We give according to our means. That is the standard for the Giving Life.

The Macedonian example in this regard would be commendable enough if it ended right here, but Paul continues saying that these generous Christians gave even "beyond their means." Now, our culture knows a thing or two about going "beyond our means." We are schooled from our earliest days in the art of spending and getting more than we can afford. There's always a financing program, always an interest rate, always a monthly payment amount that whispers: why not?

These Macedonians heard a different whisper. When the opportunity to give toward a worthy need came up, they just couldn't help themselves. Even when it meant tightening their belts, they were too excited to be a part of God's work to miss out on this once-in-a-lifetime opportunity to give!

---

2. 1 Corinthians 16:1-2

What would it look like for us to give according to our means? What would it look like for us to decide to give beyond our means? Would you ever consider proportionate giving? This is the Giving Life.

Looking Back:

1. What do you think of Paul's idea of "proportionate giving"? Is this something that would impact your level of generosity?
2. Comment on or consider this sentence above: "They were too excited to be a part of God's work to miss out on this once-in-a-lifetime opportunity to give!"

". . .of their own accord. . ."
2 Corinthians 8:3

. . . .

7. NO PRESSURE

". . . of their own accord . . ." 2 Corinthians 8:3

. . . .

So, what made these Macedonian churches so intentional and sacrificial in their giving? As we've read, they gave because they had received God's grace. The Giving Life was a natural overflow of what God had given them.

In truth, giving doesn't come naturally to us. Because of innate selfishness and human sin, we desire to take, to cling, to have, to hold, and to hoard, instead of give. But there is a way to learn to give and it is so simple that even a child can do it. And often they do!

How do we learn to give? We learn to give by giving. It is that simple. Practice makes perfect. This is perhaps the most well-kept secret of Christian generosity. When we give to others, it doesn't just impact those who will receive—it has a transforming, sanctifying effect on our own hearts!

This is what led the Macedonian churches to give "of their own accord" and even consider it a favor to be able to offer their gifts. They didn't see their condition of poverty as an excuse not to be generous; they saw it as an opportunity to increase their reliance on Jesus.

We ought to realize that Paul had enough clout, or we might say *'chutzpah'* to command people to give. He was their founding pastor; he was the church planter extraordinaire. He was famous in his own day. But he did not command. Incredibly, he leaves it to the people to determine their own financial response to the need in Judea.

One of the most amazing statements of Paul is made here. As direct as he is that people *should* give, he stops short of demanding or describing *what* they should. He says this twice. Once here, that the Macedonians gave of their own accord (and that was a good thing!). And then again, as a further instruction to the Corinthians in 9:7:

> *Each one must give as he has decided in his heart, not reluctantly or under compulsion.*

You might think with all the good-natured competition and comparative giving between the two bodies of believers, Paul might issue a stinging command: Now, therefore, do this! But he doesn't. In fact, the final arbiter of what people give rests on the very personal, heart-felt decision of the giver. That is surprising! But in a way, it is wonderful. It is refreshing. It causes our giving to be a matter of the heart.

The pressure is off! Right? The minister at the church is not allowed to apply pressure or coercion with us, according to Paul. The congregational leadership is not allowed to send an invoice for dues or membership fees in our church. There is not threat of expulsion if we do nothing or do less than we are able. There is to be NO compulsion. There is no demand.

And at the same time, for our part, there shouldn't be any reluctance from us. As we consider and decide what we can and will give, it must be because we *want* to give.

Are you thinking, "Where's the catch?" There is only one: that you and I must decide in our own hearts. We don't give according to what just happens to be in our wallets. We must think it through and decide!

Looking Back:

1. The essay above states that giving does not come naturally to us. Do you believe this? If so, how did you learn to give?
2. Paul is telling the people in Corinth that they must decide in their hearts what to give. How would this impact or change the way you give?

"Begging us earnestly
for the favor of taking
part in the relief of the
saints." 2 Corinthians 8:4

. . . .

8. COERCION OR CONVERSION?

"Begging us earnestly for the favor of taking part in the relief of the saints." 2 Corinthians 8:4

As disciples, we are called to give up our self-reliance. When we give up, the gospel can go out to the world, but grace can also come into our hearts and begin its work in us.

For many, giving is only ever externally motivated. That's not necessarily a bad thing; after all, our awareness of the needs around us should prompt us to be generous with what God has given us. But the Giving Life involves another component to Christian generosity that must not be overlooked. When we receive the grace of Jesus Christ, it works on our hearts to undo our default posture of self-ishness and bend us toward habits of loving generosity. We aren't just sitting around waiting for the needs of the world to press us into service; instead, we actively seek out ways to be Christlike by our giving.

The Giving Life is about being connected to the work that God has done *in* our life in such a way that giving is a natural outflow *from* our life. Once we embrace the Giving

Life, giving comes naturally; it might more accurately be called supernaturally.

Are you looking for a shorthand way of understanding this principle? Here is the perfect statement that describes the philosophy of the Apostle Paul.

Giving is not prompted by coercion;
it is prompted by conversion.

Boom! Think about that statement as it applies to your life for a moment. Does it change things around for you? When I first said this quote out loud, I thought it was a homophone! "Coercion/Conversion." They sound so similar. But when we let the truth of that statement sink in, we can start to see the freedom and the joy of being able to give and give generously. Generous giving comes from our conversion to Christ.

Paul wasn't twisting arms or laying guilt trips on these churches. The Macedonians had tasted and seen that this new way—The Giving Life—was good, and they began to "beg . . . earnestly for the favor of taking part in the relief of the saints." Following their example, we are called to view giving for the needs of others not as an obligation that will make our lives worse, but as a chance to participate in the vital work of God's kingdom.

In fact, their conversion drove their participation in giving to the point that they were "begging" the Apostles to give. Can you imagine that? That is what the Giving Life is—it is the reality that my conversion (not coercion) should guide and direct my understanding and practice of generosity and giving.

Looking Back:

1. In your own words, why would the Macedonians "beg" for the chance to give to the churches in Judea?
2. What if we saw giving as less of an obligation and more of an opportunity?

". . .and this, not as we expected, but they gave themselves first to the Lord and then by the will of God to us." 2 Corinthians 8:5

. . . .

9. UNBELIEVABLE!

". . .and this, not as we expected, but they gave themselves first to the Lord and then by the will of God to us."
2 Corinthians 8:5

. . . .

Consider how silly the Macedonian Christians must have looked to their friends and neighbors. Their cities were afflicted with these unknown trials, and everyone was experiencing crippling poverty. While everyone was stockpiling what little they had, here are the Christians sending off their cash to some folks they've never even met. Imagine what their financial advisors must have been telling them about this decision!

The Giving Life is bound to sound ridiculous to others. Paul understood that as he wrote this letter to the Corinthians, explaining how the Macedonians had given. In verse three, Paul interjects: "as I can testify." It is as if Paul is saying, No! Really! I saw it with my own eyes. A moment later, he reiterates again that their giving was "not as we expected." He is writing defensively, as if he imagines his Corinthian audience rolling their eyes at this fabulous tale of the impoverished Macedonians who gave with smiles on their faces. This sort of giving sounds too good to be true.

Exactly.

We have received a gospel that outshines any fairy tale. We have received a grace too outrageous to believe. Do you believe this? Be careful how you answer that question because your answer will shake things up.

Here is what I mean. If we believe that we have received an amazing grace and a gospel that outshines any fairy tale imaginable, then our giving shouldn't look any different. We haven't received the sensible, budgeted mercy of God— we've received extravagant love! Our world could use love like that from us. That doesn't necessarily mean we will be able to add extra zeros onto our checks to the church. Goodness knows the Macedonian churches weren't giving eye-popping sums. But they gave the way God gave— beyond anything we could have expected.

When others speak about our generosity, they should find themselves having to work to convince their audience. No! Really! I saw it with my own eyes!

Here is another way to look at it. If the people you know and admire in your life were to stumble across your annual giving statement to your church, what would they say? What would they think? Again, you are not giving to impress anyone, but the question is a good one to answer. Would they be blown away by your generosity? Would it challenge their own personal standards of generosity? Or not?

Looking Back:

1. What is the main point of this brief essay? Describe it or reiterate it in your own terms.
2. What do you think of this question: "If the people you know and admire in your life were to stumble across your annual giving statement to your church, what would they say?"

But as you excel in
everything—in faith, in
speech, in knowledge,
in all earnestness . . .
2 Corinthians 8:7

. . . .

10. THE "GO-GETTERS"

But as you excel in everything—in faith, in speech, in knowledge, in all earnestness . . . 2 Corinthians 8:7

The city of Corinth sat at a nexus for all sorts of trade in the ancient world; it was a thriving hub and its people filled it with constant hubbub. If you look at a map you will see that it was located on a unique isthmus—a narrow body of land with navigable water on each side. In other words, Corinth had two seaports on opposite ends of the city! The ancient city was the center of cosmopolitan life in the ancient world. And, as we know from history, Corinthians were high achievers; they were in the middle of the action in the ancient world.

Paul confirms that in their church life, the Corinthian Christians were much the same. He acknowledges that they "excel in everything." In our own culture of achievement, many of us would wish for such a phrase on our tombstones. Paul lists the Corinthian church's achievements "in faith, in speech, in knowledge, in all earnestness, and in your love for us."[3] They know what they believe, they speak out boldly, they have integrity and a loving unity with others—any pastor would be glad to take credit for such a church. They are living their mission; they are doing it all.

In other words, they were "Go-Getters"!

However, for Paul, this striving after excellence was incomplete (see 2 Corinthians 8:6). Without generosity, they were in danger of falling in love with their own achievements. But as it turns out, giving is a way that we can guard against loving ourselves to a fault. Giving defuses our inclination to turn even our spirituality into a way of proving how great we are.

In a way, it is easy to be impressed with ourselves. In many of our communities we have abundant opportunities. We have access to free education, excellent career paths, weather-proofed housing, safe communities, abundant stores of food, and other blessings of our modern era. Despite the significant challenges that everyone faces today, we are living longer and with more vitality than at any other time in history.

Paul would recognize all of this and give thanks to God for it. But he might also tap the brakes a bit and ask us who we must thank for this abundance. Where do our rights and our freedom originate? After all, aren't we just the blessed recipients of this abundance? How can we claim that any of it is warranted? We will see this issue raised in the next chapter.

---

3. ESV has "in our love for you" with this alternate meaning in a footnote. Even still, the affection is mutual.

Looking Back:

1. How does generosity keep us from falling in love with ourselves and our accomplishments?

2. What are the abundant blessings that you have been given in your life so far?

"But as you excel
in everything . . . in
our love for you . . ."
2 Corinthians 8:7

. . . .

11. FAKING IT?

"But as you excel in everything . . . in our love for you . . ."
2 Corinthians 8:7

Today's church is often labeled as hypocritical. Maybe it isn't always a fair charge, but the surrounding culture looks at what we do and say and thinks: *phony*. In a way, that charge is an easy one to level at any organization. Oftentimes our stated ideals are just that: ideals. Few people live up to the best version of themselves all the time.

However, generosity—true, open-handed, loving generosity—is one way that we can win the argument about integrity. Christians talk a lot about serving and giving and helping—about sacrificial love for the sake of others—and being genuinely generous is the one sure way to prove it. We can talk about the attributes of a faithful Christian, but when we give, we put our money where our mouth is. Literally.

Paul would agree vehemently. We see the list of excellent qualities from the Corinthian church in this passage: faith, speech, knowledge, even earnestness and love. But when you think about it, all those things can be faked!

We've all encountered believers who pretended to have it all figured out or who knew the right things to say or who seemed like they were sincere only to discover that it was all just skin deep.

And we have all done it ourselves! Haven't we? We have tried to put on airs to impress other people; maybe they were impressed. We have tried to sound impressive (speech); maybe it worked. We have pretended to be earnest. The examples are too numerous in our life to be proud of, but they all point to the same fact: *it is easy to fake most every aspect of the Christian life.*

Except generosity. Giving is the one aspect of our Christian life that proves itself true by its action.

Paul says to the Corinthians that the call to give is the call to prove that their love is genuine. He isn't trying to give them a command to be generous; such a command would never work. Instead, Paul's exhortation to give is in the best interest of the Corinthian church—only by giving will they be able to verify the authenticity of their faith to the world.

Because you can't fake generosity: it's either there or it isn't. The Giving Life is either real or it is no life at all.

In the Sermon on the Mount, Jesus makes this pretty clear: "Where your treasure is, there your heart will be also" (Matthew 6:21). John makes this more explicit when he says: "If anyone has the world's goods and sees his brother in need, yet closes his heart against him, how does God's love abide in him? Little children, let us not love in word or talk but in deed and in truth" (1 John 3:17–18). The Bible is clear about generosity: it reveals our heart, and it can't be faked.

Looking Back:

1. How could widespread generosity from Christians help the public witness of the church in the culture today? Explain.

2. Is it true that you cannot fake generosity? How would giving prove the Christian faith?

"But as you excel in everything . . . see that you excel in this act of grace also." 2 Corinthians 8:7

. . . .

12. BUILDING TOWERS

"But as you excel in everything . . . see that you excel in this act of grace also." 2 Corinthians 8:7

Paul is not admonishing the Corinthians for their excellence, but he is concerned that in striving only to excel, that they will run in the wrong direction, away from their mission. Remember the Tower of Babel from Genesis 11. In this scene, we see humans excelling in everything—organization and communication and engineering—but all those efforts are no longer moving toward building a loving community of people worshiping God. Instead, all that creative energy has been warped into a race to the top. They aren't trying to create what is true, honorable, just, pure, lovely, commendable, to use Paul's list in Philippians 4:8. They are trying to prove that *they* are the best—even better than God. Left to our own devices, we will always follow our foolish hearts into this trap.

But the Giving Life changes us in this way. We need something to cut us down to size, to remind us that we were made first and foremost to bow down. We are not to be the sole overseers of our life; we are instead to be overseen. God is watching over us and has given us the privileges and opportunities we enjoy today.

This is what acts of generosity do. Even when we operate with the best of intentions, without even trying, we heap up achievements and seek to outstrip those around us. We find ourselves building towers of our own. But the Giving Life takes all the energy of our excellence and gives it away before it heaps up around us. Generosity also counteracts our tendency to think that our excellence comes from our own doing. Twice Paul repeats his desire that the Corinthians would participate in "this act of grace." In other words, to know and understand that the good things we have and the good things we do come from God.

Go back to the Tower of Babel story and ask what would have made the difference. If you read the story from Genesis 11, you might come away with the notion that pride, self-promotion and boasting are the inevitable result of great achievements and progress. According to the biblical account, they are!

However, there is one thing that can act as an antidote to runaway pride and self-promotion: generosity. When we are caught up in the Giving Life, it is harder to get caught up in our life!

Try it sometime. When you are feeling overly impressed with yourself and your accomplishments, take a little bit of your time or money and give it away to someone who might need it. Look with compassion at the less fortunate and needy. Look at them through the eyes of Christ. Try to see them as He sees them, and you will find that your own generosity has humbled you.

Looking Back:

1. How do our achievements pose a spiritual danger for us and our assessment of ourselves?

2. Go to Genesis 11 and review the account of the Tower of Babel with this in mind: How have you seen similar attitudes to the Babylonians who were more focused on their personal success than growing closer to God?

"For you know the grace of our Lord Jesus Christ, that though he was rich, yet for your sake he became poor, so that you by his poverty might become rich." 2 Corinthians 8:9

. . . .

13. RAISING OUR EYES

"For you know the grace of our Lord Jesus Christ, that though he was rich, yet for your sake he became poor, so that you by his poverty might become rich." 2 Corinthians 8:9

In verse nine, Paul changes his argument. He redirects his Corinthian audience from looking toward the example of their sister churches and instead points them to the example of Jesus: "For you know the grace of our Lord Jesus Christ."

This is an intentional turn for Paul. Up to this point, he's been asking them to think of themselves in relation to others and he's stirred up their already-present desire to excel in everything. Now, he pulls the rug out from under them. He knows that it would be dangerous for them to remain in this mindset of comparison. Their ambitions should stir them up but not allow them to wallow in self-absorption. So, Paul reframes the whole conversation on generosity by showing them a new standard. Here is his point: we should measure our giving, we should measure our generosity, not in relation to others, but by the generosity of God. It is good for us to be inspired by the generosity of others, but we can't let that become our only standard. We need to raise our eyes up.

This is a whole new standard for us. There are no more competitive drills or cheers with the Macedonians. Paul did that just to get their attention. There are no more appeals to greatness or glory in giving. Paul is winning his argument one point at a time. Paul's point now is about the most genuine of all reasons to give—we should look up to Jesus and what He did. That should be our main reason for giving.

We give because God gave. We reach others because God reached us. This call to give like God isn't just about raising the bar—it is about becoming a part of a bigger story than the one we've been writing. When we give, we aren't just being polite or practicing a good habit. We aren't trying to become "the best version of ourselves," and we certainly aren't trying to prove ourselves better than anyone around us. The mission is bigger than that. When we give, we are recklessly pursuing the generous way of Jesus. We are drawing near to the very nature of God himself.

Our thoughts should linger on this idea for a few minutes. If our purpose in following Jesus is to become like Him as much as we can, one of the first things we will start to practice is giving. To become a disciple of Jesus is to become a giver. The Giving Life is the Christian Life and vice versa.

Looking Back:

1. In what ways is Jesus the model and exemplar of giving and generosity?

2. What do you think of this statement: "To become a disciple of Jesus is to become a giver"?

"And in this matter I give my judgment: this benefits you, who a year ago started not only to do this work but also to desire to do it." 1 Corinthians 8:10

. . . .

14. AN INCREASE OF DESIRE

"And in this matter I give my judgment: this benefits you, who a year ago started not only to do this work but also to desire to do it." 1 Corinthians 8:10

I f we want our hearts to be formed after God's own heart, then it starts with giving. Often, we convince ourselves that transformation is an inside-out process. First, we fix who we are on the inside through some deep, spiritual process, and then we will begin to act more and more like Christ in our daily lives. In our linear world where things happen in a straight line, this can make sense.

But on this issue, Paul raises the question: what if it's a two-way street? What if right now—before you learned how to pray like a pro and before you'd memorized the New Testament—you began to practice giving? What if you gave according to your means and then even beyond your means? What if you gave generously to the church and to those in need? What if you cleared out time in your schedule and gave that away to help others?

In other words, what if we are changed on the inside and the outside at the same time? What we do affects how we feel; what we feel impacts what we do. This is the miracle of personal change that comes to those who are part of the Giving Life. As we give generously, we become the kind of person who gives generously. Do you believe this? If you don't, I dare say that you can prove it to yourself by simply giving.

Paul argues that once you begin to do the work of giving, you will find that you begin also to desire to do it. The act of doing something good and right on the outside impacts our internal and emotional world on the inside. What if you started imitating the character of God before you "felt" like it or felt ready or worthy to do it? What if you recognized that you'll never be worthy—that all good works begin with God's act of grace? Paul's argument is that as you give, your desire to know Christ more and draw nearer to him will increase.

This may sound like "fake-it-till-you-make-it" language, the very sort of thing that leads the church to be accused of hypocrisy. But generosity can't be faked. Unlike other virtues, even our half-hearted or unwilling efforts, make the same impact as the perfectly and purely motivated ones. God asks us to give generously, trusting that when we step into the life he has for us, we will find joy and fulfillment where we least expected.

Looking Back:

1. In the second paragraph above, there are a series of questions. How would you answer them for your life?

2. What would it mean for you and your family to embrace and practice the Giving Life?

"So now finish doing it as well, so that your readiness in desiring it may be matched by your completing it out of what you have."
2 Corinthians 8:11

. . . .

15. PERSEVERING TO THE END

"So now finish doing it as well, so that your readiness in desiring it may be matched by your completing it out of what you have." 2 Corinthians 8:11

All of us have those unfinished projects that haunt us. The half-organized garage. The guitar that was abandoned a few years ago after learning only a few chords. An empty, blank journal that we bought long ago in which to write our innermost thoughts. As much as our lives are marked by our achievements, they are also dotted with what we didn't complete.

Paul urges his Corinthian brothers and sisters to carry on the task of giving to completion. They are ambitious, high-achieving people; undoubtedly, they will hear Paul's words and immediately set to work. But will it last? What does it take to be generous for the long haul?

For some, it will be a matter of practical habit-making. Many of us excitedly give on Sunday mornings as an act of worship but mailing a check each month feels tedious and boring, so our generosity is only as steady as our often-sporadic church attendance. Every church has online giving options, and they work fine. But the problem with that method is that it automates giving; we end up not thinking about the very thing that should be at the top of our minds: what can we give for the benefit of God's mission?

Many of us get excited about causes. We attend a fundraiser or banquet, and we are impacted by the slideshows and testimonies, and our wallets fall open easily. But the everyday needs slip our minds and slip out of our budget.

For others, there's something more spiritual happening when we are unable to sustain our giving over time. We become like the plants that spring up in the rocky soil but wither when the sun comes up, because we have no root (Mark 4:3–9). When we find ourselves frustrated by our own lack of perseverance in giving, we should take an inventory of our prayer and Bible study and submit ourselves again to the task of following in Jesus' footsteps.

This is when we would be wise to hear the counsel and encouragement of Paul: "so now finish it as well." This is loving counsel from a man who cares for these Christians in Corinth like the pastor who has brought each of them to faith. And he has. He loves them all, and his words should not be read as a scolding master of the house, but as a fellow follower of Jesus Christ.

It does raise a good question though, doesn't it? Of all the causes we care about, of all the missionaries we said we would support, of all the intentions to give and support the church that we have had—what needs finishing now?

Looking Back:

1. Do you have unfinished commitments or half-finished projects? What prevented you from completing the task?

2. Paul loves the Christians in the church in Corinth. He is not shaming them; he is shepherding them in the faith. What would he say to you in this matter?

"For I do not mean that others should be eased and you burdened, but that as a matter of fairness your abundance at the present time should supply their need, so that their abundance may supply your need, that there may be fairness."
2 Corinthians 8:13-14

16. "BLESS THEIR HEARTS"

"For I do not mean that others should be eased and you burdened, but that as a matter of fairness your abundance at the present time should supply their need, so that their abundance may supply your need, that there may be fairness."
2 Corinthians 8:13–14

The Corinthian church obviously had the financial resources to provide relief to those suffering in Judea. They must have heard about the dire needs that were so far away and thought to themselves: "Well, bless their hearts."

I have lived in Texas for nearly forty years. When I first arrived, I heard people at the church use that expression. I thought they were empathetic, but many times I learned that the phrase was a way of dismissing others. I learned that the well-worn Southern phrase was often used as a polite screen for our sense of superiority and a spirit of condescension. Sometimes our pity for people warps into thinking of them as pitiful people. People who aren't as successful as we are. People who aren't as clever as we are. We think of ourselves reaching down from on high to pull up those hopeless souls from the depths of despair.

But Paul paints a different picture of the situation, and it's rooted in the grace of Jesus. The good news of the gospel is that it is offered to all of us because all of us need it. None of us have pulled ourselves up by our own bootstraps. None of us washed our own sins away. While we were sinners, Christ died for us (Romans 5:8).

But here is the way Paul wants us to feel about it: we do not offer our generosity to those in need because we are *saviors*, but because we are *saved*. Yes, our present abundance can supply a present need for someone else, but we could never imagine ourselves so high and mighty that we won't one day need help ourselves. We give—especially among our brothers and sisters in Christ—out of a spirit of reciprocity, knowing our equal need of grace and equal standing in the eyes of God.

Looking Back:

1. What is this chapter saying about the intentions in our own heart as we give for the benefit of others?
2. How can pride or condescension ruin giving for the sake of others?

"Each one must give as he has decided in his heart, not reluctantly or under compulsion."
2 Corinthians 9:7

. . . .

17. A MATTER OF THE HEART

"Each one must give as he has decided in his heart, not reluctantly or under compulsion." 2 Corinthians 9:7

Talking about money is necessarily personal, especially given our financial culture today. Christians shouldn't have to post their bank account holdings on the church website or publish giving totals by each family in the Sunday bulletin. Jesus insists throughout his ministry that giving should be done without any ostentatious show. In fact, our Lord blasted those generous Pharisees as show-offs because they trumpeted their giving with, well, trumpets! Jesus is crystal clear about this aspect of giving: Giving should be done so secretly that your left hand should not know what your right hand is doing! (Matthew 6:3)

Each person should decide in his own heart what to give. And, as we saw earlier, that means that pastors and church leaders should exert no pressure. But neither should someone else's giving influence your own. As Paul indicated about the Macedonians, let the fact that they gave what they decided to give be enough to encourage you to give what you have decided to give.

It would be so much easier if we were each told what to give, like a tax. Or what if a church established the budgeted needs for the congregation and divided that by the number of people in the church? Each person would be assessed a "fair share." That might be easy to calculate, but it would take the heart out of giving altogether. Every member would receive an invoice!

That would not be right. Why? Because sacrifice means something different to every individual and family. Seasons of life will dictate what generosity will look like during certain ages and stages of life. And we need to be prepared to give one another grace to discern, decide, and then love and support them as they grow toward Christ through their giving.

Giving to the mission of God through the church is a deeply communal experience. It's a beautiful expression of our shared commitment to God and to one another. But it starts in every individual's heart. We can't apply a "one-size-fits-all" giving plan as the only way to model Christian generosity. It's a recipe for coercion and guilt, which sounds more like the way of the Pharisee than the way of Jesus. When we talk about giving with one another, and even as we seek to encourage one another to increasing faithfulness in our financial lives, we must look at it as an invitation to discipleship that must be accepted in its own way.

Looking Back:

1. What is the problem with "reluctant" giving?
2. What is the difference between "fair share" giving and "proportionate giving"?

" . . . for God loves
a cheerful giver . . ."
2 Corinthians 9:7

. . . .

18. CHEERFUL

". . . for God loves a cheerful giver . . ." 2 Corinthians 9:7

We've heard it a thousand times before the plate is passed on Sunday mornings: "God loves a cheerful giver." Maybe for you these words have become cliché, or maybe they've even become coercive—perhaps the pastor's voice has had a little edge to it: God loves a cheerful giver, so let's see some smiles out there, people!

What does it mean to give cheerfully? Some leaders, trying to exert pressure or influence upon our financial commitment, will tell us to give till it hurts. That usually means that we should give what we had planned but add even more until it starts to hurt our net worth.

But that is not the Giving Life at all. Paul's instruction is the opposite. He says that we should give until it feels good! Or until we feel good about it. Give until our gift gives us something to cheer about! God loves that! He loves when we are a "cheerful giver."

But what does it mean that God loves when we give gladly? Doesn't God always love His children? Does He not love us when we are unable to give or when we find giving difficult?

Let's be very clear: of course, God always loves His children, no matter what we do.

But any parent knows the swelling of pride and delight that comes when their child does something beautiful. It isn't the same pride we might feel if our child hit the game-winning home run or got an 'A' on a big test. No, this is the kind of love that fills our heart when we see our children follow the path we've set for them, when they model the virtues we've hoped we could pass down to them. When they are kind to someone who is different. When they forgive their sibling. When they persevere even after they fail.

God loves when His children step into the way of life that He has laid out for us. It breaks His heart to watch His sons and daughters reject His goodness and chase after their own self-destruction. When we give to others with hearts filled with joy, God rejoices that we are becoming more and more His children, marked by the 'family values' of the Trinity.

This is the fruit of the Giving Life. When we give, we become like the One who gave His life for us! We take on the attributes of the Lord of all history.

Looking Back:

1. We have all heard the expression "give until it hurts." Paul says that we should give until we become a "cheerful giver." How is this an important distinction?
2. What is your response to the last paragraph of this chapter?

"And God is able to make all grace abound to you, so that having all sufficiency in all things at all times, you may abound in every good work." 2 Corinthians 9:9

19. ALL ABOUNDING

"And God is able to make all grace abound to you, so that having all sufficiency in all things at all times, you may abound in every good work." 2 Corinthians 9:9

Here in verse nine, Paul uses the word *all* four times. He paints an appealing picture, a picture of fullness and possibility that counters the emptiness and helplessness that we so often feel in our lives. Most of the time, we want to do the kind of "good work" Paul is talking about. But we imagine that it will come at a price to our checkbook, to our calendars, and to our energy level. Doing "good work" sounds terribly exhausting.

Paul writes to the Corinthians that it doesn't have to be this way. God is a God of abundance, and there is a way to be fully equipped, fully able in all situations to do the work that he has given us to do. And it starts with grace.

In other words, the Giving Life is not a zero-sum game. When we give of our time, talent, or financial resources, we are not diminished. There is not "less" of us because we gave some of us away. It is just the opposite. God returns it all . . . and then some!

But how does that work? Let's drill down into this strange spiritual phenomenon.

Paul's formula here is the same one we find in 1 John 4:19: "We love because he first loved us." Our work is enabled, empowered, and inspired by the grace that has been given to us. That's why Paul has been so insistent that the gift from the Corinthians is not given "reluctantly or under compulsion" but that it instead needs to be decided in each person's heart (2 Corinthians 9:7).

Generosity has the unique ability to build in us an understanding of the grace we have received, and once that has happened, that same grace can "abound" in us, filling up our insufficiencies and sending us out to do good work in the world.

Looking Back:

1. What does it mean that the Giving Life is not a "zero-sum" game? How does that expression apply?
2. Have you ever experienced an abundance of supply that came from giving? What happened?

"He who supplies seed to the sower and bread for food will supply and multiply your seed for sowing." 2 Corinthians 9:10

. . . .

20. REAL PROSPERITY

"He who supplies seed to the sower and bread for
food will supply and multiply your seed for sowing."
2 Corinthians 9:10

. . . .

This verse and indeed this whole metaphor about seed has been the victim of much bad theology over the years. This metaphor has been enlisted by the so-called "prosperity gospel." It is insidious and is the cause of much silliness, suffering, and scandal in the church.

The argument of the prosperity gospel goes something like this:

God doesn't want His children to be unhappy, and when we don't have money, we are unhappy. So, even though God asks us to give our money away, He promises that once we do that, He will give us even more money than we had in the first place. That's why we should give.

At first glance, you could see that sort of thinking here in 2 Corinthians 9:10. After all, Paul does promise that God will multiply our seed. But look closer. When we give, what are we promised to receive? Not bread—something that we enjoy and consume. We receive seed—something that is put right back to use.

Do you see the difference between giving bread and receiving seed in return? Paul is saying that when we give money, we do not receive money in return. Our gifts do not always put God on the hook to give us that same thing in kind. Instead, we receive what we need to make more bread—more seed.

The promise isn't that once we've been generous, then God will let us be selfish. The promise is that when we give, we will find ourselves living squarely in the middle of God's will for our lives, and that God will give us more and more opportunities to participate in His work.

This is the Giving Life. God will always provide for our needs. Jesus makes that plain in the Lord's Prayer and the Sermon on the Mount. But when we give, we usually aren't rewarded with second helpings; instead, we are given more and more chances to work alongside our Savior.

Looking Back:

1. What is the Prosperity Gospel? How does this chapter address it?
2. How has God supplied your needs in the past?

"You will be enriched
in every way to be
generous in every way."
2 Corinthians 9:11

. . . .

21. THE BEAUTIFUL CYCLE

"You will be enriched in every way to be generous in every way." 2 Corinthians 9:11

. . . .

We all like the idea of being enriched. I'm sure many of us have heard or seen a few promises this week that we could get rich quick if only we follow certain advice.

From the previous chapter, that there were exclusions to the bread and seed formula that Paul mentions in verse 10. Most of the time when we give bread, we get seed in return. But I can't explain why this is not always the case. Ask anyone in your church who has given "bread"—money, time, talent—and they will likely tell you a story of God miraculous provision of the same. It happens. This kind of miracle provision—bread for bread—is a reality to be enjoyed, not expected or demanded. God is not a slot machine waiting for you to put in something so that he can dispense something more.

As we've been exploring this teaching from Paul, we've learned that the promise of God to those who give generously isn't the kind of enrichment we might have looked for. Paul writes that we will be enriched in every way to be generous in every way. It's a beautiful cycle that begins with the grace that we've received that we offer out toward others through our generosity. God blesses our faithfulness, increases our desire, and creates more and more chances for us to be a part of the work.

God's promise isn't just limited to our finances because our call to generosity isn't just limited to our finances. God calls us to be generous in *every* way. That means we are to be generous to those who steal our parking spots at the grocery store, generous to our spouses when they disagree with us, generous with our bosses who don't appreciate our work. Generosity is bigger than money, and so is God's promise to enrich and equip us. When we open our eyes to the big story of God's generosity, we will find enrichment far beyond our bank accounts.

The Giving Life is not filled with efforts and energy when we give to receive. That cannot be our motivation. That kind of giving has nothing to do with the Christian faith. That is Las Vegas. But the truth is that when we give as an act of worship, we step into a divine relationship with an active and living God. And the truth is that we never can know where that relationship will take us; we never know how that relationship will bless us. But we can trust that it will.

Looking Back:

1. What is the author unable to explain? Read the second paragraph. Has this phenomenon been true in your own life?

2. Why is giving more in order to get more antithetical to Paul's understanding of the Giving Life?

"For the ministry of this service is not only supplying the needs of the saints but is also overflowing in many thanksgivings to God." 2 Corinthians 9:12

22. HEARTS OF WORSHIP

"For the ministry of this service is not only supplying the needs of the saints but is also overflowing in many thanksgivings to God." 2 Corinthians 9:12

So far in this series of meditations and commentary, we've talked about how giving is far more than basic charity. Christians give to meet the needs that we see around us, but our mission isn't limited to a simple utilitarian goal. We've seen how giving is at the heart of discipleship, shaping us more into the generous image of Jesus.

Here, Paul pulls back the curtain even further, revealing that ultimate goal of our giving is the worship of God. The Giving Life is really a life of worship.

Of course, we've always known that giving is part of our worship; after all, we collect the morning's offering during our worship service, or we have arranged for weekly transactions online. But we maybe don't realize that this is true on an apocalyptic level. In the book of Revelation, we get a glimpse of where all things are headed. The end of time culminates in the beautiful vision of God being worshiped in all His glory forever and ever. The purpose of all creation from the very beginning has been to fulfill that vision, to bring glory and worship to the Triune God who is worthy.

When we give, our hearts are placed in a posture of worship. When we give, we join the song of all creation that acknowledges and praises God as Lord of all. And it doesn't stop with us. When we give to others, we show forth God's goodness so that others can see and join in as well. In Paul's words, giving creates "an overflow of thanksgivings to God."

Looking Back:

1. How is the act of giving like the act of worship? What challenges does online giving pose for the church today?

2. How does your church encourage people to give as part of their worship experience?

". . .because of the surpassing grace of God upon you. Thanks be to God for his inexpressible gift!"
2 Corinthians 9:14–15

. . . .

23. PURSUING CHRIST

". . .because of the surpassing grace of God upon you. Thanks be to God for his inexpressible gift!" 2 Corinthians 9:14–15

A s we close out this deep dive into Paul's letter to the Corinthians, we can say a final word about Paul and his view of our life in Christ. Again and again in his letters, Paul describes the Christian life in terms of chasing after something. We run to reach a prize (1 Corinthians 9:24, Philippians 3:14). We endure (2 Timothy 2:12). We reach (Colossians 2:2). We flee youthful passions and pursue righteousness (2 Timothy 2:22).

The imagery of pursuit extends back to the Israelites, following a pillar of cloud by day and a pillar of fire by night. It extends back to Jacob who wrestled with God in pursuit of his blessing. It extends back to Abram, who followed the voice of a God he'd never known to a place he'd never been.

We are called to pursue the life of Jesus. And the truth that Paul arrives at after all his encouragement to the Corinthians is the beautiful reminder that we can never outstrip the generous love of our savior. The grace that He has given us will always go before us. It surpasses even our most ambitious offerings. To some, this may seem like bad news. It may seem to reinforce a narrative we rehearse too often: a story of falling short—of not measuring up.

That's just the point, though. We were never pursuing the generosity of Jesus so that we could prove ourselves worthy. We weren't pursuing Him so we could be perfect. We were pursuing Him because He gave us life; He gave us hope; He gave us an inexpressible gift we could never have earned or deserved. And that's someone worth following.

Looking Back:

1. How are we called to make an effort to follow Christ and yet not think we are earning anything by following Christ?
2. What kind of effort are you willing to make in your faith when it comes to generosity?

24. CONCLUSION

When Paul started his work in the city, he was fearful. Perhaps he felt defeated because his preaching, teaching, and missionary efforts in Athens had failed to produce a new church, much less a single convert.

Then, one night in a dream, Paul heard from the Lord that He (the Lord) had people in the city. These people were to become the first members of the new church. The Lord said, *"Do not be afraid, but go on speaking and do not be silent, for I am with you, and no one will attack you to harm you, for I have many in this city who are my people."*[4] Paul must have breathed a sigh of relief knowing that God's people were present in the city. Thus, Paul stayed in Corinth for 18 months to work among the people and plant the now-famous Corinthian church.

We can conclude that Paul's labor among the Corinthians was a labor of love. His instructions and corrections which so often are regarded as hard words from the Apostle, should be read in this light. He loved the people of this church. He wanted God's best for them. He knew

---

4. Acts 18:9-10

that many (or most, if not all) of them were living colorful, worldly lives and that the gospel had called them to a higher pursuit. And, as we have seen in these two chapters from his second letter, God was calling them to the Giving Life.

What does this mean for us today?

We can hope that Paul might write our modern churches with the same love and devotion that he had for the Corinthians. He might urge us toward acts of love, highest moral living, right use of spiritual gifts, unity among members, proper understanding of marriage, and correct doctrine about prophecy, worship, and the resurrection of the dead. We would expect all these instructions and warnings and more from the great Apostle.

And from the two chapters of Second Corinthians that we have studied, we can also conclude that Paul would also call us to the Giving Life. He would give us a clear and compelling vision about how to use the money, time, and resources we have for the strengthening of the Body of Christ—to meet the needs of the church and of the people in need wherever we find them.

The Giving Life is the life of every Christian. Or rather, it should be. This is the clear teaching of the New Testament. Still, the choice we have in living this way rests solely upon us. We cannot be coerced to give or to be a giver. We cannot be pressured, shamed, cajoled, or guilted into generosity. Paul would urge us, as he did 2000 years ago. He would encourage us, as he did in his church in Corinth. But, in the end, it will rest upon what each Christian believer and each faithful family will decide to give.

It is a biblical puzzle that there is only one thing that Paul says in Acts or writes in his letters that is a direct quote of the Lord Jesus Christ. Only one thing. And we can let this widely-known statement of Jesus that was repeated by Paul and remembered by the early church—we can let this statement be Paul's final word to us about the Giving Life. "It is more blessed to give than to receive" (Acts 20:35).

DAVID ROSEBERRY is an ordained Anglican priest and has been in ministry for nearly 40 years. He was founding Rector of Christ Church in Plano for over 30 years and now is the founding director of LeaderWorks, a non-profit ministry that serves churches and church leaders. He is a speaker, writer, teacher, and minister at large for the Anglican Church in North America. David Roseberry lives north of Dallas with his wife, Fran.

David Roseberry has a coaching practice that equips pastors for the complex role of leadership in their congregatons. In addition, he consults with churches, boards, and non-profit organizations to help them refine or renew their mission and ministry. You can contact David directly at LeaderWorks: David@LeaderWorks.org.

David's books are helping laypeople and ordained leaders grow deep in their faith and the practice of ministry. Please search "David Roseberry" on Amazon for a current list of titles. As of the printing of this book, David's work includes these titles.

- **When the Lord is My Shepherd** is a deep dive into the most famous poem in the Bible, the 23rd Psalm. David wrote this book during the early stages of the pandemic. It is a line-by-line study of this short, beautiful Psalm.

- **The Ordinary Ways of God** is an in-depth study of the Book of Ruth and the fascinating characters in it. The book is designed for individual study or group use.

- **The Psalm on the Cross** is a series of devotional reflections and commentary on our Lord's Passion and His use of Psalm 22 at Calvary. Line by line, verse by verse, the Psalm tells the story of the crucifixion and the hope of redemption through the Cross. This book is perfect for personal daily devotion, group study, or congregational use during Lent.

- **Giving Up** is David's first book written for ordained and congregational leaders. The book will help any leader of any detonation understand biblical stewardship and give practical tips and program advice for increasing generosity and stewardship in the local congregation.

- **The Rector and the Vestry** is a book for Anglican clergy and lay leaders. Churches and leaders have used this book to help train members of the electing board called Vestry.
- **A Field Guide for Giving: How to Increase Generosity and Stewardship in the Local Church** will help pastors and leaders avoid hazards, appreciate the divine landscapes, and safely navigate the challenging trails as you lead and teach stewardship and generosity.

David is a speaker, preacher, and teacher and can be invited to speak at church services or conferences. Please email him at David@LeaderWorks.org to inquire about dates.

David and his wife Fran lead life-changing trips to Israel and other places of the Christian faith. For over three decades, they have guided and hosted tours to the Holy Land, having toured the land well over 30 times. You are welcome to join them on their trip. Consult the LeaderWorks website for travel dates, destinations and opportunities.

The Giving Life can be purchased in cartons of 50 copies for a discounted price. This special price will help congregations buy copies for their entire membership. Contact info@leaderworks.org for more information and to place an order